Hurricane Katrina

DISASTER ALERT!

Ellen Rodger

Crabtree Publishing Company
www.crabtreebooks.com

presented by:

Crabtree Publishing Company
www.crabtreebooks.com

For those with untold stories...

Project editor: Carrie Gleason

Editors: Rachel Eagen, Adrianna Morganelli, L. Michelle Nielsen

Book design and production coordinator: Rosie Gowsell

Production assistant: Samara Parent

Scanning technician: Arlene Arch-Wilson

Art Director: Rob MacGregor

Photo research: Allison Napier

Research: Rosie Gowsell

Photographs: AP/Wide World Photos: cover, p. 12 (bottom), p. 14, p. 15 (bottom), p. 16, p. 17 (bottom), p. 18, p. 19 (top), p. 20 (top), p. 22 (top), p. 23 (bottom), p. 24, p. 25 (both), p. 26, p. 27 (both), p. 28 (top), p. 29 (top); Corbis: p. 5; Tim Johnson/Reuters/Corbis: p. 19 (bottom); Gerardo Mora/epa/Corbis: p. 1; Petty Officer Kyle Niemi/epa/Corbis: p. 4; NOAA/Corbis: p. 7; Jim Reed/Corbis: p. 15 (top); John Riley/epa/Corbis: p. 3; David J. Phillip/Pool/Reuters/Corbis: p. 17 (top); Mike Theiss/Jim Reed Photography/Corbis: p. 12 (top); Irwin Thompson/Dallas Morning News/Corbis: p. 20 (bottom), p. 21 (bottom); FEMA News Photo:

p. 23 (top); Jez Coulson/Insight/Panos Pictures: p. 28 (middle); NOAA/Photo Researchers, Inc.: p. 11; Reuters/Lee Celano: p. 22 (bottom); Reuters/Marc Serota: p. 21 (top); Reuters/Rick Wilking RTW/fa: p. 13 (bottom); Other images from stock photo cd.

Illustrations: Dan Pressman: p. 6, p. 8; David Wysotski, Allure Illustrations: pp 30-31

Cartography: Jim Chernishenko: p. 10

Cover: A U.S. Navy helicopter rescues people from a rooftop. Flood waters in New Orleans rose so high in parts of the city that people were forced into their attics and onto their roofs, where they awaited rescue.

Title page: A New Orleans graveyard flooded by Hurricane Katrina.

Contents: Hundreds of thousands of people were evacuated from New Orleans before and following Hurricane Katrina. Many found shelter at the Houston Astrodome, in neighboring Texas.

Library and Archives Canada Cataloguing in Publication
Rodger, Ellen
  Hurricane Katrina / Ellen Rodger.

(Disaster alert!)
Includes index.
ISBN-13: 978-0-7787-1586-3 (bound)
ISBN-13: 978-0-7787-1618-1 (pbk)
ISBN-10: 0-7787-1586-8 (bound)
ISBN-10: 0-7787-1618-X (pbk)

  1. Hurricane Katrina, 2005--Juvenile literature. 2. Hurricanes-- Juvenile literature. 3. Disaster victims--United States--Juvenile literature. 4. Disaster relief--United States--Juvenile literature. 5. Rescue work--United States--Juvenile literature. I. Title. II. Series.

HV636.2005.U6R63 2006   j363.34'9220976   C2006-905190-9

Library of Congress Cataloging-in-Publication Data

Rodger, Ellen.
  Hurricane Katrina! / written by Ellen Rodger.
    p. cm. -- (Disaster alert!)
  Includes index.
  ISBN-13: 978-0-7787-1586-3 (rlb)
  ISBN-10: 0-7787-1586-8 (rlb)
  ISBN-13: 978-0-7787-1618-1 (pbk)
  ISBN-10: 0-7787-1618-X (pbk)
  1. Hurricane Katrina, 2005--Juvenile literature. 2. Hurricanes--Juvenile literature. 3. Disaster victims--United States--Juvenile literature. 4. Rescue work--United States--Juvenile literature. I. Title. II. Series.

QC945.R63 2006
976'.044--dc22   2006029176

Crabtree Publishing Company
www.crabtreebooks.com   1-800-387-7650

Published in Canada
Crabtree Publishing
616 Welland Ave.
St. Catharines, ON
L2M 5V6

Published in the United States
Crabtree Publishing
PMB16A
350 Fifth Ave., Suite 3308
New York, NY 10118

Published in the United Kingdom
Crabtree Publishing
White Cross Mills
High Town, Lancaster
LA1 4XS

Published in Australia
Crabtree Publishing
386 Mt. Alexander Rd.
Ascot Vale (Melbourne)
VIC 3032

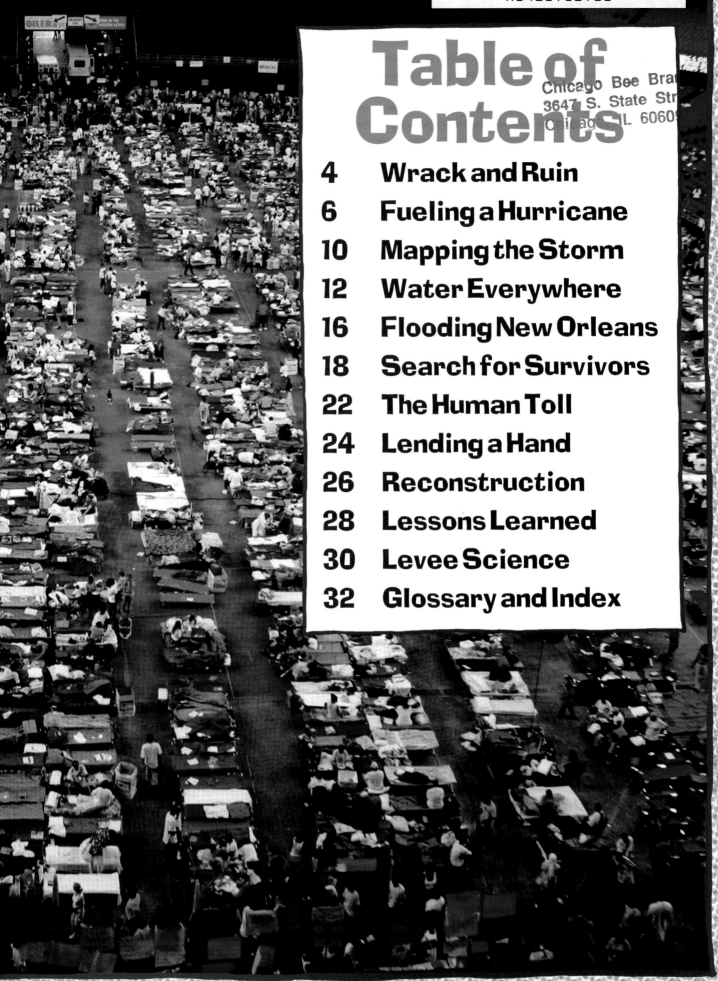

Table of Contents

Wrack and Ruin

Hurricane Katrina was the most destructive natural disaster ever to hit the United States. The massive and powerful storm swept through parts of Florida, the Gulf coast of Louisiana, and Mississippi in August 2005.

New Orleans, Louisiana, 2005

What is a disaster?
A disaster is a destructive event that affects the natural world and human communities. Some disasters are predictable and others occur without warning. Coping successfully with a disaster often depends on a community's preparation.

Hurricane season

Each summer, powerful ocean-born storms called hurricanes batter the Atlantic coast of North America, the Caribbean, and the Gulf of Mexico. Hurricane Katrina was the fourth major storm of the 2005 hurricane season. Katrina devastated many communities, resulting in the most costly storm recovery effort ever in the United States.

(above) Rescue workers used helicopters to airlift people from the roofs of their flooded homes.

Waters and warnings

Katrina killed an estimated 1,800 people and brought storm surges and floods that destroyed or flooded many communities, including the nearly 300-year-old city of New Orleans, Louisiana. A storm surge happens when storms at sea cause the water level to rise higher than normal, and water spills onto land. Despite warnings that a major hurricane would hit the area, many people could not or would not **evacuate** their homes. By the time a **mandatory** evacuation was issued for New Orleans, it was too late. Those who stayed had nowhere to go or no money or cars to leave with.

(below) French settlers built the first artificial levees along the Mississippi River in New Orleans in the 1700s. Since that time, 1,000 miles (1,609 kilometers) of levee have been added to protect lands along the river.

When the levee breaks

The Mississippi River has one of the longest levee systems in the world. Levees are embankments made along the edge of a river to protect against seasonal floods. River flooding has breached the levees several times. In the great Mississippi flood of 1927, heavy rain forced flood waters over the levees, covering thousands of miles of land. Hundreds of people drowned and thousands were left homeless. People were sent to relief camps and many African Americans were forced at gunpoint to work in flood relief and levee building. The flood was an inspiration for many folk and blues songs that detailed hardships and the fear of a levee "breaking" or failing.

Fueling a Hurricane

Hurricanes begin as ocean storms in tropical regions, just above and below the Earth's equator. Certain conditions must be present for a hurricane to develop.

Hurricane power

Ocean water must be 80° Fahrenheit (26° Celsius) or warmer to create the energy needed to power a hurricane. Water heated by warm air over the ocean's surface creates water vapor. Water vapor is a gas that rises up and **condenses**, or turns into droplets of water that fall back down as rain. This cycle of rising water vapor and falling water droplets repeats itself over and over, releasing heat energy. The heat then warms the air over the ocean surface and causes it to rise, and cooler air rushes in to take its place, creating a pattern of wind.

Building pressure

For a hurricane to develop, an area of high pressure must exist in the **atmosphere** above the storm. Air pressure, or atmospheric pressure, is the weight of air pushing down on Earth. Cold air has more weight, so it makes up an area of high pressure. Warm air is lighter, so it has low pressure. An area of low pressure is located near the ocean's surface. Air naturally moves from an area of high pressure to an area of low pressure. The greater the difference between the high and low pressure areas, the stronger the moving air, or wind. Hurricane winds are "fed" by this rapid exchange of air from an area of high to an area of low pressure.

How water fuels a hurricane

1. Heat from the Sun warms the ocean water, which begins to evaporate, or become a gas.
2. The water vapor rises with warm air (red arrows) while cooler air (blue arrows) from the atmosphere above replaces it. This creates spinning winds.
3. Water vapor cools as it rises and condenses into clouds and falls back down as rain.
4. As the cycle repeats itself, more energy is released. Strong winds form and pull more warm air and water from the surface to help the hurricane grow.

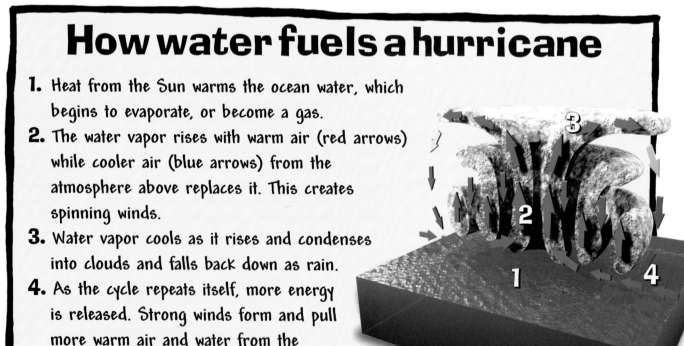

Hurricane Katrina, August 28, 2005, Gulf of Mexico

Wind systems

Converging winds must also be present for a hurricane to form. Converging winds are winds that come together, or meet. During the summer months in the Atlantic Ocean, two "belts" of wind located just north and south of the equator, called the **trade winds**, converge. The place where they meet is called the intertropical convergence zone. This is where many of the world's tropical thunderstorms develop. When these storms group together, they sometimes develop a vortex, or rapidly spinning whorl. The grouped storms become hurricanes when they gather strength and travel over warm oceans.

This satellite photo shows what Hurricane Katrina looked like from space. In the Northern Hemisphere, winds in a hurricane spin in a counterclockwise direction around a calm center called an eye. The winds move in this direction because of the Coriolis force, which is caused by the rotation of the Earth on its axis. As the Earth rotates under the atmosphere, the winds are forced to curve. The Coriolis force causes winds to deflect to the right in the Northern Hemisphere, and to the left in the Southern Hemisphere.

How a hurricane forms

1. Tropical disturbance

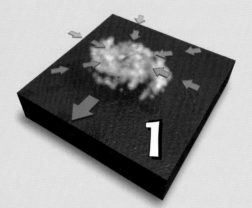

A hurricane begins as a tropical disturbance. This occurs when thunderclouds gather into a cluster over tropical waters around a center of low pressure. Winds during a tropical disturbance move at less than 23 miles per hour (37 kilometers per hour).

2. Tropical depression

When the air pressure in a tropical disturbance drops, winds begin moving in a cyclonic, or swirling, pattern. Tropical depressions have surface wind speeds from 23 to 38 miles per hour (37 to 62 kilometers per hour). At this stage of development, swirling winds start to rotate around a center.

3. Tropical storm

A tropical storm is slightly weaker than a hurricane, and will develop into a hurricane if air conditions change. Tropical storms have swirling winds with speeds of 39 to 73 miles per hour (63 to 118 kilometers per hour). At this stage, the storm is named.

4. Hurricane

When the winds of a tropical storm reach 74 miles per hour (119 kilometers per hour), it becomes a hurricane. The winds are organized around a well-defined center, called the eye. Hurricanes are downgraded back to tropical storms and tropical depressions as they move further inland and become weaker.

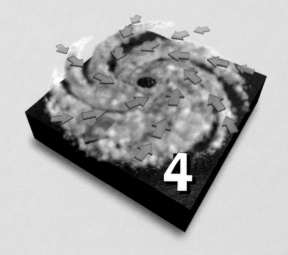

Hurricane scale

When television or radio weather forecasters talk about a hurricane's strength, they usually rate it on a scale of one to five. That scale is called the Saffir-Simpson hurricane scale. The Saffir-Simpson scale measures intensity based on a storm's wind speed. A Category 1 hurricane has winds of 74 to 95 miles per hour (119 to 153 kilometers per hour) and can cause slight damage to trees and signs. A Category 2 hurricane has winds of 96 to 110 miles per hour (154 to 177 kilometers per hour).

A Category 3 hurricane has winds of 111 to 130 miles per hour (179 to 209 kilometers per hour) and can destroy mobile homes and knock trees down. A Category 4 hurricane has winds of 131 to 155 miles per hour (211 to 249 kilometers per hour). It can cause severe structural damage to homes and cut off escape routes near the coasts. A Category 5 hurricane has winds greater than 155 miles per hour (249 kilometers per hour) and can destroy entire buildings.

"Driving" more hurricanes?

Climatologists are scientists who study weather patterns over a long period of time. Some climatologists believe hurricanes are becoming stronger and more destructive because ocean temperatures are warmer as a result of global warming. Global warming is the gradual warming of the Earth's atmosphere caused by burning fossil fuels. Fossil fuels such as oil, natural gas, and coal are used to heat and cool homes and businesses, and to run automobiles and airplanes. They give off gases that trap the Sun's heat in the atmosphere. This extra heat raises ocean temperatures. High ocean water temperatures are needed for hurricanes to form.

Pollution created by burning fossil fuels contributes to global warming.

Mapping the Storm

August 30, 2005
Hurricane Katrina is downgraded to a tropical depression

6

Kentucky

Tennessee

Mississippi

Alabama

Hurricane Katrina began on August 23, 2005, as a tropical depression in the Atlantic Ocean. During the course of a week, it grew in size and strength, and moved into the Gulf of Mexico. Use this map to track Katrina's path of destruction. Match the numbers on the map with those on the opposite page.

Louisiana

5

Atlantic Ocean

Florida

August 29, 2005
Hurricane Katrina makes landfall in Louisiana and Mississippi as a Category 3 hurricane

New Orleans

August 25, 2005
Katrina hits Florida as a Category 1 hurricane

August 24, 2005
Tropical Storm Katrina

3

2

4

Gulf of Mexico

1

August 27-28, 2005
On August 27 the storm is designated a Category 3 hurricane. The next day, Katrina again gains strength and becomes a Category 4, and then, only hours later in the same day, a massive Category 5 storm

August 23, 2005
Tropical Depression

CUBA

MEXICO

Storm tracking:

1. Warmer than usual ocean water, and the remains of another storm helped create Tropical Depression Twelve over the Bahamas.

2. Tropical Depression Twelve became a tropical storm and was given the name Katrina.

3. Katrina became a Category 1 hurricane and raged across south Florida, killing 10 people. Winds and rain caused power lines to go down and flooded some areas.

4. Katrina lost strength after passing over Florida, but gained it again in the warm waters of the Gulf of Mexico. **States of emergencies** had been declared a day earlier in Louisiana and Mississippi. Gulf of Mexico oil platforms were evacuated and fishing fleets grounded.

5. The hurricane made landfall in Louisiana. It brought rain and winds as high as 130 miles per hour (209 kilometers per hour) and a storm surge of 20 feet (six meters) that flooded much of New Orleans. Flood waters also took over parts of Alabama.

6. The storm lost energy as it traveled north over land. In the Gulf states, thousands of people had been killed and entire communities destroyed.

NOAA sends aircraft up into hurricanes to measure air pressure, wind direction, and wind speed. Inside the hurricane's eye, the winds are calm.

Watchers

The National Hurricane Center (NHC) is part of the National Oceanic and Atmospheric Administration (NOAA), a federal government agency that monitors and studies weather, climate, the ocean, and environmental issues. The NHC and the National Weather Center track, or follow, hurricanes from their beginnings and keep a record of hurricane history. They also make predictions, based on scientific study, for each year's hurricane season. The NOAA's National Hurricane Center issues hurricane advisories, which notify residents of certain areas when a hurricane is coming their way.

Eye of Hurricane Katrina, August 28, 2005

Water Everywhere

Residents of southern coastal states live with the constant knowledge that hurricanes are dangerous. Some years bring a dozen or more of the killer storms. With each storm comes warnings to evacuate and head for higher ground.

Fort Lauderdale, Florida, August 25, 2005

Below sea level

The destruction brought by Hurricane Katrina was made worse because of where the storm made landfall. Many cities and towns in parts of southeast Louisiana and Mississippi are below sea level. Sea level is the level of the ocean's surface between high and low tide. When the storm surge hit and the water was pushed ashore, it washed away properties for many miles inland because there was no higher ground to keep homes safe. As Hurricane Katrina crossed Florida, several areas were severely flooded. When it hit Louisiana and Mississippi, entire communities were swamped.

(above) When Hurricane Katrina hit southeast Florida, it brought wind gusts of over 80 miles per hour (129 kilometers per hour).

(below) A man begs for help after being stranded by the storm. Many people ignored the evacuation warnings, or had no way to get out.

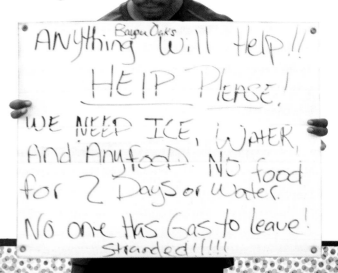

Warnings and orders

Even before the hurricane touched land, government officials and disaster relief agencies were afraid of the damage Katrina would do. The **Gulf Coast states** began preparing for Katrina on August 25, the day the hurricane made landfall in Florida. Several levels of government were involved in a complicated **emergency response** and evacuation system. Emergency response system messages were sent out on television and radio, and emergency response centers and shelters were opened. By August 27, people living in Mississippi and Louisiana were told by their local governments to evacuate, or leave the area. Traffic lanes coming into New Orleans were reversed to outbound, so more people could drive out of the city. By August 28, the mayor of New Orleans issued a mandatory evacuation order, which would force people to leave their homes. What some government officials did not plan for was that many residents did not have the money or transportation to leave, even if they wanted to.

(below) Hurricane evacuation signs line highways of some Gulf Coast states.

HURRICANE EVACUATION ROUTE

New Orleans, Louisiana, August 28, 2005

The day before the storm hit Louisiana, highways were jam-packed with people fleeing New Orleans. Hundreds of thousands of residents were ordered to leave the city.

Soaking in it

The city of New Orleans opened the Superdome football stadium to residents fleeing the storm, but warned them to bring their own food, water, and blankets. The Louisiana **National Guard** brought 13,000 bottles of water and meals to the stadium. An estimated 12,000 or more people weathered the storm in the stadium. Outside the stadium, the city was nearly destroyed by the hurricane. Thousands of people who had not found shelter were killed in the storm. Bodies floated in flooded city streets after the storm. Many homes were flattened and taller buildings had their windows blown out. Parts of New Orleans were completely covered with water when the levees that protect the city were **overtopped** or **breached** by the storm surge. Power was cut and the sewage system was overrun, spewing raw sewage into the flooded streets. The waters took weeks to recede.

Gulf Coast nightmare

Other Gulf Coast communities were also nearly destroyed. The high winds and storm surge that swept through Biloxi, Mississippi, leveled most of the city's buildings near the coast and heavily damaged others. Over 50 people in Biloxi were killed by the storm. Some Mississippi communities, such as Gulfport and Waveland, were nearly wiped off the map and had very few buildings left standing after the hurricane swept through. Houses were blown apart by the fierceness of Katrina's winds. Debris such as tables and televisions and other household goods were strewn everywhere. Even trees were stripped of their leaves and bark.

The Louisiana National Guard rescued city residents and brought them to the Superdome after Hurricane Katrina hit in New Orleans. The Superdome was a center of last resort.

Seeking refuge

Millions of people who lived on the Gulf Coast fled to evacuation centers in other cities and states. The centers, which were often gymnasiums, provided food and a place to sleep on cots or on the floor, next to other people who had to leave their homes. Most of the evacuation centers were temporary. People who lost their homes, or could not return because of floodwaters, spent months in motels or trailers provided for a time by the Federal Emergency Management Agency (FEMA).

Gulfport, Mississippi, August 29, 2005

Hurricane Katrina hit Mississippi as a Category 3 hurricane and destroyed many communities.

FEMA's role

The Federal Emergency Management Agency (FEMA) is a government agency that helps the country prepare and recover from disasters. FEMA delivered water and ice to hurricane centers and put emergency response teams on alert while Katrina was churning in the Gulf of Mexico. Before Katrina made landfall, FEMA also set up staging areas that held trailers and equipment, such as bulldozers, and supplies, such as water and prepared meals called Meals Ready to Eat, or MREs. FEMA was criticized in the weeks and months after the hurricane for not acting quickly enough to help evacuate people, or come to their aid after the hurricane.

FEMA could not handle the enormous task of looking after disaster relief. Months following the storm, trailers were still being shipped by FEMA to the South.

Flooding New Orleans

New Orleans is a port city surrounded by water. Even before the storm, most experts agreed that the levees surrounding the city could not withstand the force of a strong hurricane.

Big bowl of water

New Orleans is only six feet (two meters) above sea level. The city is shaped like a giant bowl, which means that once water passes the level of the levees and flows into the city streets, it has no way of draining out naturally, and must be pumped out. Hurricane Katrina's high winds, heavy rain, and storm surge forced water over and through several levees and flood walls surrounding the city. Many pumping stations, which pumped the water back out, failed because they could not cope with the volume of water. The resulting floods covered 80 percent of New Orleans. Many areas of the city were flooded by over 20 feet (six meters) of water.

The Mississippi River lies to the south of New Orleans, Lake Pontchartrain to the north, and Lake Borgne and the Gulf of Mexico to the east. Over the years, a system of levees was built to protect New Orleans from the waters that surround it. During Hurricane Katrina, many levees failed and the water flowed into the city.

Near downtown New Orleans, September 1, 2005

Power outages prevented many of the levee pumping stations from pumping storm water back to Lake Pontchartrain. Since telephone service was also down, officials could not communicate with each other to make reports on levees.

Protection system

New Orleans has flooded before, but never on the scale of what Hurricane Katrina brought. Hurricane Betsy flooded parts of the city in 1965, and Hurricane Camille, in 1969, also nearly stretched the levee system to the breaking point. With each threat, the New Orleans Flood and Hurricane Protection System was improved. The system includes 350 miles (563 kilometers) of levees, **floodwalls**, bridges, gates, and canals, that direct water away from the city. If one levee fails, the other surrounding levees can withstand the added pressure of the floodwaters. After Katrina, several levees failed or were breached or overtopped. This overwhelmed the flood protection system and led to the massive flooding.

(right) City residents make their way down a flooded New Orleans street.

Search for Survivors

After the storm subsided, search and rescue operations began. Police officers, firefighters, the Coast Guard, the military, and volunteers went out in helicopters and boats to rescue people who had survived the hurricane.

Plucked from rooftops

Many people did not evacuate their homes or reach shelters before or during the storm. These people were forced to ride out the storm in their homes or another safe place. After the storm, the Coast Guard is believed to have rescued 33,000 people from their flooded homes and even from trees. Some people were pulled to safety by volunteers who brought their own boats and plied the flooded streets looking for survivors. Most survivors were brought to shelters. In the confusion of the rescue effort, some were simply dropped on dry land, including closed highways, where they waited again to be rescued.

New Orleans, September 1, 2005

People who stayed in their homes headed for higher ground after the floodwaters started to enter their houses. Eventually making it onto what remained of rooftops, people waited for days for rescue helicopters to save them. People survived on the food and clean water they had in their homes prior to the storm hitting.

Superdome survivors

Television footage of the days after the hurricane showed the world how desperate things were in New Orleans. At the Superdome football stadium, where many took refuge from Hurricane Katrina, thousands of people spent days awaiting help, unable to leave. Thousands more people came to the stadium for help after venturing out from their homes to the flooded streets. The stadium was without power and running water. Three days after the hurricane made landfall, rescuers began evacuating people from the Superdome. People waited days to be bussed to the Houston Astrodome in Houston, Texas, and locations in other states.

(above) For days people lived in the cramped, dirty conditions of the Louisiana Superdome

More than a million people fled to evacuation centers in other states and cities before the hurricane. Many of these centers were temporary shelters set up in gymnasiums and stadiums.

Exodus

The New Orleans Convention Center, and the Interstate-10 highway became other temporary homes to people fleeing their own flooded homes. It took a week to evacuate the Convention Center, where people lived in very hot, cramped conditions without water or food for a time. While most people were heading to higher ground, some people were looting stores, carrying off mostly the food and water they needed to survive.

(below) People ended up stranded at the Convention Center and on Interstate-10 because there was nowhere else for rescuers to drop them off. The Superdome and other evacuation centers had reached capacity.

A Coast Guard official rescues two children from the Ernest N. Morial Convention Center. Aid was not sent to people who had taken refuge there until September 1, when conditions in the center were deemed unsafe and unsanitary.

(above) While trying to evacuate prisoners from a Louisiana prison, a highway floods and leaves the inmates and their guards stranded.

Delays and confusion

Much of the difficulty in rescuing people and bringing them to safety after Hurricane Katrina, was caused by the rescue and relief agencies being unprepared for such a disaster. The city, state, and national governments were involved with the disaster declaration and relief efforts. Government protocols, or rules, on what agencies were supposed to provide, caused further confusion and delay. Often, people were rescued or given assistance by ordinary citizens and non-governmental agencies such as charities and churches.

Taking refuge

In the days after the storm, the media described evacuees as "refugees in their own country." What the media meant was the people forced to leave their homes were experiencing some of the same hardships as refugees fleeing war or terror. Most evacuees came to evacuation centers in other cities and states with small bags. Some had less than 30 minutes to get their most necessary belongings together before they were brought to safety. They left behind their loved ones, friends, pets, jobs, and possessions. Evacuation centers provided food, a place to sleep on cots on the floor, and a safe place to stay for a short period. Afterwards, most of Katrina's victims could not return home because home no longer existed or was contaminated by polluted water. Over many weeks, they were shifted to more permanent living quarters in other areas of the country where they picked up the pieces of their lives and waited for housing to be built in their destroyed communities.

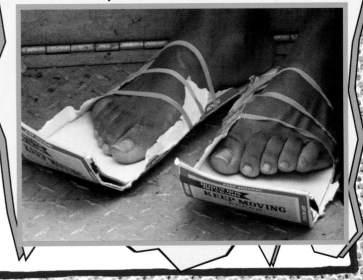

The Human Toll

As the days and weeks went by, rescue efforts were replaced with recovery efforts. When the floodwaters were finally pumped out of New Orleans, people went house to house searching for bodies.

Forced separation

In the confusion before the hurricane, some New Orleans families were separated as some family members headed for evacuation centers and others stayed in their homes. After the storm, flooded city streets made it impossible to check on family and friends. Electricity and telephone lines were knocked down and few people had boats to ply the streets of their city. Once at evacuation centers, people could not leave to return home. In some cases, children separated from their parents after going to different evacuation centers were not reunited for weeks or even months. In their haste to leave, many evacuees left behind their identification documents, so they could not prove who they were. Nobody knew how long it would be before they could return but nobody expected it would be months or years.

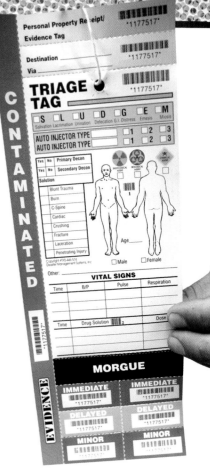

(above) Triage tags were worn by the injured to show their condition until more help arrived.

Houses were searched for bodies and marked with a giant X, but even this system was not foolproof. Some bodies were overlooked in the first searches because searchers did not look everywhere or failed to sift through debris. Searching was difficult work. Each house often took up to half a day to search. Workers never knew what they would find.

Re-building a life

Hurricane Katrina evacuees were relocated all over the country. Most stayed as close to home as possible, at first in shelters, then hotels, trailers, or apartments provided by relief agencies. Katrina hit at the beginning of the school year. Schoolchildren had to re-enroll in other schools and their parents struggled to find jobs to begin their lives again. Losing their homes meant losing everything they had known before. Daily tasks such as washing, cooking, playing games, and even sewing a button on a shirt, were made impossible because people had nothing left.

(right) A dog searches for the scent of human bodies in a flood-destroyed home.

The death toll

The death toll from Hurricane Katrina may never be fully known. Over 1,800 people have been confirmed dead and another 1,600 or more are still missing. Months after the hurricane, bodies were still being found. Most of the people killed by Hurricane Katrina drowned in the floods that overtook New Orleans during and after the storm. Many of those who died were elderly, ill, African American, and poor. They drowned in their homes, as rising floodwaters gave them no way to escape. In hard-hit areas outside New Orleans, people were killed by the storm as it crushed their houses, blew them away, or flooded them out.

Bodies of people who had died during the hurricane were left on streets until people could come and collect them. Families of the dead sometimes waited months before they heard that their loved ones were dead.

Lending a Hand

Recovering from a disaster the size and scope of Hurricane Katrina is a slow process. Recovery workers and volunteers worked for months to help survivors. Most had training through agencies such as the Red Cross. Without the help of volunteers, the devastation would have been much worse.

New Orleans, Louisiana, September 11, 2005

Weeks after the hurricane hit, some areas of Louisiana were still flooded. Rescue teams came from across North America to help search for survivors, such as this Search and Rescue team from San Diego, California.

Volunteer workers

Many volunteers, people with a wide variety of skills such as truck driving, nursing, or cooking, were sent to disaster recovery centers throughout Texas, Mississippi, Louisiana, and Alabama. Doctors and emergency medical workers came to assist with the sick. Volunteers helped cook food to feed survivors and the thousands of workers assisting in the recovery effort. They handed out supplies such as water, diapers, bug spray, and even mops to people cleaning up their flooded homes.

Volunteer agencies

Disaster relief agencies provided food, shelter, and money to victims of Hurricane Katrina. Evacuees were encouraged to register with FEMA or the American Red Cross so that they could receive emergency aid. Billions of dollars were spent helping people. Churches in neighboring states also provided support, sending relief workers and money, and giving evacuees a place to live and time to recover. Some volunteer groups even helped people clean their mucky, flood-damaged homes.

Far from home

The impact of Katrina will be felt for many years. Some people forced out of their homes will never return. They have found new homes and jobs in other communities. The state of Texas opened its schools to new students whose homes and schools had been destroyed by the hurricane. Students at closed or damaged New Orleans area universities and colleges were accepted at other schools across the country so that they could continue to learn.

(left) Immediately following the hurricane, people in many states held drives for food, supplies, and clothing to be sent to Katrina survivors.

Helping pets

Thousands of victims who fled the floods were forced to leave behind their pets because rescuers only had room for humans. These pets were left to fend for themselves. Many drowned or died from lack of food and fresh water. Animal welfare organizations helped rescue pets, as well as wild animals displaced by the flood. Many pets were not reunited with their owners and some owners are still looking for their animals. Shelters in New Orleans evacuated their animals before the storm. Shelters also gathered as many scared and abandoned pets as they could in the days and weeks after the hurricane. They fed them, washed them, and gave them medical care. Some shelters put animals they rescued after Hurricane Katrina up for adoption.

(above) Pictures of animals with missing owners were posted at an emergency animal shelter in Louisiana. The state passed a law in June 2006 that now allows pets to be evacuated with their owners.

Reconstruction

Rebuilding the areas hit hard by Hurricane Katrina has been a slow process costing billions of dollars. Everything from homes, to businesses, hospitals, and levees has to be remade or rebuilt.

New Orleans, Louisiana, 2005

Homes? What homes?

More than a year after the hurricane, many New Orleans residents still had not returned home. The flood and hurricane winds had damaged their homes so severely that they could not be repaired. Mold, rot, and the terrible smell of sewage, death, and decay had made their homes unfit to live in. Other New Orleans residents moved to the upper floors of their homes while waiting for main floors to be repaired. Many people lived with holes in their roofs and musty smelling walls. The **Army Corps of Engineers** and FEMA provided homeowners with blue tarps to cover holes in hurricane-damaged roofs to keep rain out while they waited for repairs.

Living in trailers

People in other Gulf Coast areas hit by the hurricane lived in cramped trailers, some for over a year, while they waited for their homes to be rebuilt. The lack of homes was so desperate that the government even had to provide money to construct buildings for workers reconstructing levees in New Orleans. Without clean, safe places for people to live, the city of New Orleans could not fully rebuild.

(above) A girl stands in front of the rubble of her New Orleans home. The house was destroyed by Katrina and then caught fire.

Bay St. Louis, Mississippi, September 3, 2005

People in many Gulf States had to dry out their homes and possessions after the hurricane to prevent mold from forming. Mold causes breathing problems, making buildings toxic to live or work in.

Help wanted

Businesses, such as restaurants and stores, that reopened in the weeks and months after the flood in New Orleans were desperate to find workers. Workers could make more money by demolishing houses. All workers were desperate to find housing. Reconstruction in parts of the city had created a construction boom.

Levee reconstruction

In the first days after the flood, workers from the city of New Orleans and the Louisiana state government tried to patch the breached levees. The Army Corps of Engineers brought in sandbags to stem the flow of water through the breaches. Once the water was drained from flooded areas of the city, the Army Corps of Engineers set about rebuilding levees and canals. The rebuilding included concrete and stone reinforcements and a new pumping system as well as restoring the **wetlands** surrounding the levees.

Repairing and reconstructing the levees cost an estimated $5 billion.

27

Lessons Learned

Hurricane Katrina was one of the worst disasters in American history. It also became an example of terrible disaster "management." Through a series of mistakes and underestimations, the disaster cost countless lives and billions of dollars.

Unprepared

Katrina became a disaster when ordinary citizens and different levels of government could not cope with the enormous scale of the destruction. The storm overwhelmed local police, fire, and emergency services. Katrina also pointed out how unprepared a wealthy country with so many resources was for a catastrophic disaster.

(above and right) Looting was a problem for homes and businesses in New Orleans after the hurricane. Some people trapped in their homes without supplies broke into stores and took what they needed.

Underestimation

From the beginning of the storm, a thorough mandatory evacuation was not carried out for vulnerable locations such as New Orleans. After the hurricane made landfall, electricity, and communication systems such as telephone, radio, and television, were knocked out. It was unclear who was responsible for rescuing people since the local and state level governments were unable to cope. People were rescued by the National Guard and by volunteers. State requests for help from the federal government went out too late, and when federal help did arrive it was poorly organized and directed in the beginning.

Some schools were cleaned up and reopened. These private school children returned to school one month after Hurricane Katrina swept through New Orleans.

Fixing things for the future

The Department of Homeland Security is the federal government department that oversees FEMA and works with other departments to provide disaster assistance and relief. Since Hurricane Katrina, the Department of Homeland Security has been working on improving its response to disasters and developing a National Preparedness System. A more organized system would help all levels of government and relief agencies work faster to rescue people, and provide them with safe shelter and the basic necessities of life. The Army Corps of Engineers is also strengthening and rebuilding the levees surrounding New Orleans in order to prevent a major flood from happening again.

Be prepared!

Recovery experts say everyone should have a disaster or emergency plan:

Talk to your family about the disasters that can occur where you live. Explain the dangers and make a plan of how to leave your home and where to meet in case of a disaster. Learn about disaster warning signals that are sent on the radio and television. Make a disaster preparation kit and place it where it can be easily grabbed in an emergency. Items to include in your kit:

* Copies of personal documents, such as birth certificates
* Flashlights and waterproof matches
* Bottled water
* A few first aid items
* A list of phone numbers of people to contact in case of emergency, including family and friends

Levee Science

These pages show how I-wall levees in New Orleans were breached and overtopped and what kinds of levees and environmental conditions are considered better able to withstand surges and floodwaters.

Flood barriers

A levee is an embanked flood barrier used to hold high water back in areas that lie close to rivers and oceans. Many conditions contribute to flooding, including how a levee is constructed, what materials it is made with, and whether there are any other barriers that can slow or stop a storm surge.

I-Wall levee

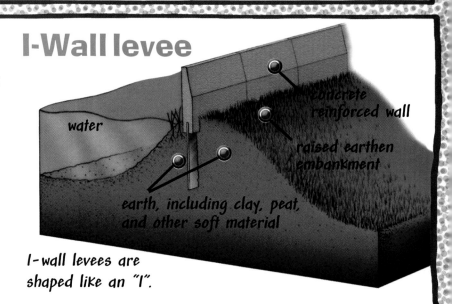

water

concrete reinforced wall

raised earthen embankment

earth, including clay, peat, and other soft material

I-wall levees are shaped like an "I".

Levee overtopped

A levee is overtopped when the water level is higher than the levee wall. The water on the side that the levee is supposed to protect wears away at the soil, weakening the earthen embankment. This leads to a breach, or break in the levee.

Levee breached

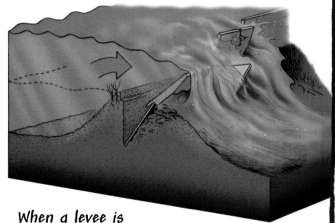

When a levee is "breached" it means it failed and was not strong enough to hold back floodwaters. Breached levees either "tip over" with the force of the water or are damaged and fall apart from overtopping.

T-Wall levee

Levee Makers

The United States Army Corps of Engineers has been building and repairing levees along the Mississippi River since the late 1800s. The Corps receives funding for levee building projects from various levels of government. After Hurricane Katrina, the Corps worked hard to repair at least four breaches in levee system canals. Levee builders think that T-wall levees are more durable.

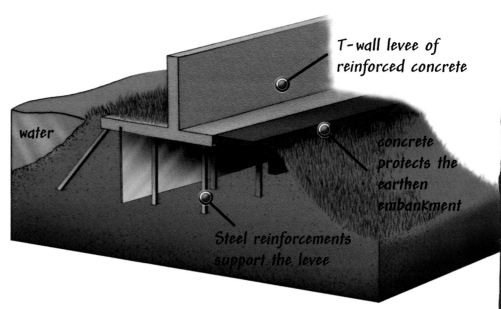

water

T-wall levee of reinforced concrete

concrete protects the earthen embankment

Steel reinforcements support the levee

The steel reinforcement walls of T-wall levees look like upside down Ts. The steel helps keep the earth pilings underneath more stable, so they are less likely to erode.

Wetlands: stopping the flood

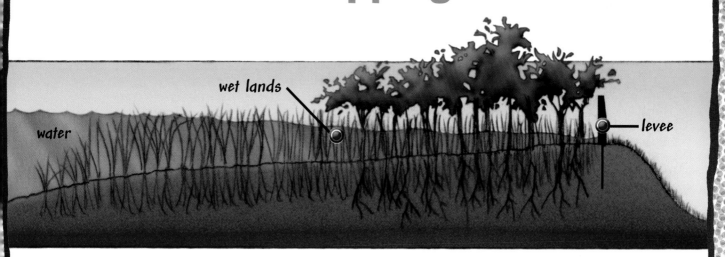

wet lands

water

levee

Conservationists believe a healthy marsh system, with well rooted trees and other vegetation, would help the levees do their job slowing an oncoming storm surge. The storm surge would first wash over the wetlands, so that by the time the water reached the levee, the water level would be much lower.

Glossary

Army Corps of Engineers A branch of the United States Army responsible for maintaining inland waterways, such as canals and rivers, and for flood control systems

atmosphere The layers of gases that surround Earth

breach An opening or hole

condense To change from a gas to a liquid

contaminated Dirty or impure

deflect To turn from a straight course

emergency response The immediate assistance given to victims of an emergency, such as a natural disaster

evacuate To leave an unsafe area

floodwall A long, tall, concrete embankment built along a body of water to protect land from floods

Gulf Coast states In the United States, the states that border the Gulf of Mexico. They are Texas, Louisiana, Mississippi, Alabama, and Florida

mandatory Something that must be done

National Guard United States military reserves that are recruited by the state, but equipped by the federal government. They can be called on by either the state governor in a state of emergency, or by the president

overtopped When floodwaters have reached the highest point of a levee and start to pour over it

refugee Someone who is forced to flee their home because of safety concerns

satellite An object in space that orbits, or moves around another object. Satellites can be natural, such as the Moon, or artificial

state of emergency A government declaration in the face of a natural disaster, war, or civil unrest that puts emergency response agencies on alert

trade winds Wind systems that blow long and steady across a certain region of the Earth

wetlands Tidal areas or swamps

Index